MW00817432

MR. POPPER'S PENGUINS

by
Richard and Florence Atwater

Teacher Guide

Written by:
Anne Troy

> ### Note
> The Dell Yearling edition of the book was used to prepare this teacher guide. The page references may differ in the hardcover or other paperback editions.

ISBN 1-56137-177-7

To order, contact your local
school supply store, or—

Table of Contents

Skills and Strategies

Thinking
Brainstorming, visualizing,
evaluating, analyzing details

Writing
Description, narrative, poetry,
journal, letter, news story

Comprehension
Predicting, sequencing,
cause/effect, inference,
comparison/contrast

Literary Elements
Character, setting, plot
development, story map,
conflict, theme

Listening/Speaking
Participation in discussion,
reader's theater, drama

Vocabulary
Synonyms, antonyms, words
in context

Novel Units, Inc.
P.O. Box 791610
San Antonio, TX 78279

Summary of *Mr. Popper's Penguins*

Mr. Popper is a house painter with an unusual winter hobby. He reads books on polar expeditions and writes letters to explorers. He writes to Admiral Drake, who sends him an Antarctic penguin whom he names Captain Cook. The penguin becomes ill and droops. After the veterinarian cannot cure Captain Cook, Mr. Popper asks the aquarium for help. They send another penguin named Greta, and soon there are ten more little penguins. Penguins eat a great many fish, and Mr. Popper does not have enough money to feed his family and the penguins. After creating a highly successful music hall act, Mr. Popper is finally able to achieve his dream of polar exploration.

About the Author

Richard Atwater taught at the University of Chicago and wrote a humorous newspaper column in verse. He married Florence H. Carroll and had two daughters. Mr. Atwater began writing *Mr. Popper's Penguins*, but when he became ill, Florence Atwater completed writing the book.

Introductory Activities and Information

Note:
It is not intended that everything presented in this guide be done. Please be selective and use discretion when choosing the activities you will do with the unit. The choices that are made should be appropriate for your use and your group of students. A wide range of activities has been provided so that individuals as well as groups may benefit.

1. Display a large globe and a flat surface map of the world. The teacher will ask the students to locate the North and South Poles and Antarctica. (See the map on the next page of this guide.)

   Not all penguins live in polar regions. They make their homes in cool waters, but no penguins go north of the equator. Cool waters exist close to the equator in the South Pacific Ocean, and penguins are found there also. Additional activities related to the map will be included in the unit.

World Map

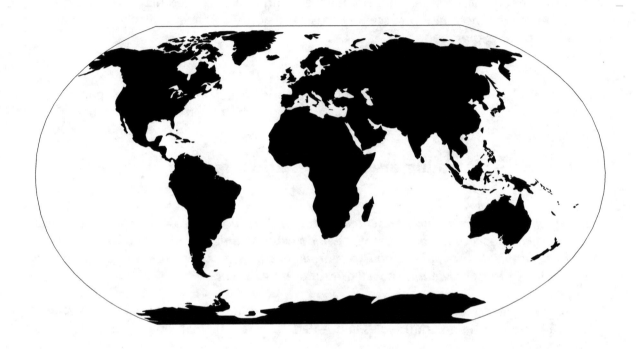

2. Brainstorm the word *Antarctica.* Possible responses:

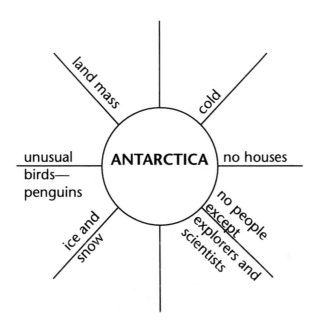

3. Prediction: Have students examine the cover illustration and title, then flip through the book. Ask: What kind of book do you suppose this will be? What is suggested by the title? Make some good guesses about this book. For example, the cover shows:

   • penguins walking on a stick or rope
   • a man in unusual clothes
   • a woman playing piano
     —She has a funny hat.
     —She is wearing gloves.
   • This is a Newbery Honor Book.

4. What is a Newbery Honor Book? *(picked by teachers and librarians as one of the best books of a certain year)* When was this book written? Find the copyright. *(1938)* What is a copyright? *(the exclusive statutory right of authors to publish and dispose of their works for a specified period of time of 28 years in the United States)*

5. Reviews and Summary: Read aloud the remarks on the back cover and the back cover summary. What does the summary tell you about what to expect from this book?

6. Prereading Discussion Topics: Encourage free, open-ended discussion on these topics, or use them as writing assignments.

Exploring Antarctica: What is an explorer? Why would anyone want to go to Antarctica? How do explorers get ready for such an expedition? What do the explorers study there?

Theater Acts: How do musical or theater acts get set up in theaters? If you had a special act, how would you get interviews? If you were very successful in local theaters, how would you get national attention?

Aquariums: Where are aquariums with penguins? Can you find information on the Internet about aquariums and penguins? If you were to talk to an aquarium or zoo director, what questions would you ask?

7. Real versus Make-Believe: Is this going to be a make-believe story or a realistic story? How do you know? Use this T-diagram to discuss.

Realistic Story	Make-Believe Story
Setting—our world	Setting—not quite our world
Characters—like us	Characters—unusual
Action—could happen	Action—never could happen
Problem—could be ours	Problem—couldn't be ours

8. Log: Have students keep a response log as they read:

In one type of log, the student pretends to be one of the characters. Writing on one side of each piece of paper, the student writes in the first person ("I..." about his/her reaction to what happened in that chapter). A partner responds to these writings on the other side of the paper, as if talking to the character.

In the dual entry log, students jot down brief summaries and reactions to each section of the novel they have read. (The first entry could be made based on a preview of the novel— a glance at the cover and a flip through the book.)

Pages   **Summary**   **Reactions**

                                    (These might begin: "I like the part..."; This reminded me of the time...")

Alternatively, as students read, they might simply jot thoughts and questions on sticky notes and apply them to the passage in question for later reference.

9. Writing: Have students freewrite for ten minutes using one of the following "starters."

- Zoo keepers…
- Penguins are…
- Animals that children like in the zoo are…
- If I could be in show business, I…

Vocabulary Activities

1. Graphic Journals
For each reading section, have students choose five to ten words whose definitions they don't know. Then let them choose from several activities to "journal" each word:

A. Word Triangle   B. Word Bug

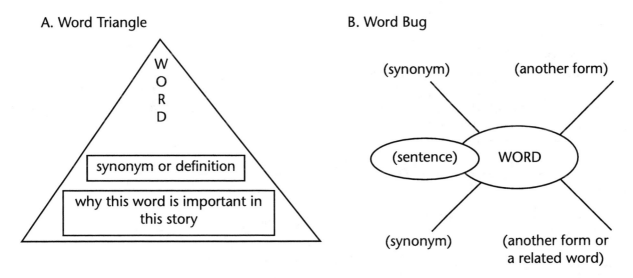

C. Word Card

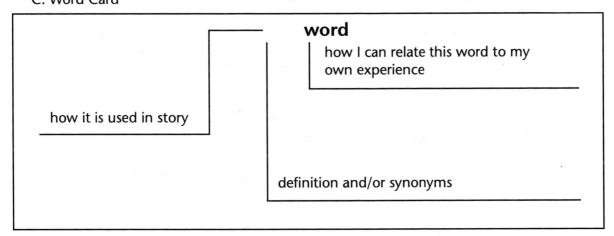

2. Venn Diagram

Use Venn diagrams which show how two words are alike and how they are different.

3. Vocabulary Log

Students keep a log of important vocabulary words (selected either by them or by you) that they meet in the story, context clues (if any), and the definition for some, but not all, of the words in the list. (Requiring students to look up every unfamiliar word is not advisable; it can be an overwhelming task.)

Word	Clues to Meaning	Dictionary Definition

4. Synonym Trains

Have students work together to create "synonym trains" and "antonym trains."

Synonym Example: **din**—noise—uproar—tumult

You might have students make synonym trains for:

　　　　erect 11　　tidy 12　　impressed 14　　promptly 36　　distinctly 42

Antonym Example: **vivid**—forgettable—colorless—bland

You might have students make antonym trains for:

　　　　reluctantly 44　　subdued 45　　reproach 49　　vigorously 53

5. Word Sort

Present students with target words for the day or week. Divide students into cooperative groups and have them sort the words into categories. (A word might go into more than one category.) A representative from each group explains the sortings to the whole class, and differences between group decisions are discussed. Categories:

WORDS THAT DESCRIBE

Things   Animals   Humans   Places   Actions

6. Mobiles

Make word mobiles using several vocabulary words related to one idea. Include pronunciation from the dictionary, location of the word in the book, how you'd use them in your everyday language, as well as a working definition.

7. Pantomime

Have students act out some of the vocabulary words and see if classmates can guess the target words.

8. Vocabulary Password

Students play in pairs, one giving the definition and the other answering. The definition-giver gets a list of words to try to get his/her partner to say. The pair of students who can guess the most words in a specified number of minutes wins.

9. Crossword Puzzles

Have students use vocabulary words from a chapter to make crossword puzzles on graph paper. They should write a question for each word and then distribute the puzzles to the other students to work out in their free time.

10. Word Maps

Develop word maps. Use color to distinguish antonyms, synonyms, etc. Display in the classroom. These may be done individually or in cooperative groups.

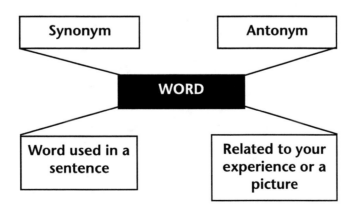

Using Predictions in the Novel Unit Approach

We all make predictions as we read—little guesses about what will happen next, how the conflict will be resolved, which details given by the author will be important to the plot, which details will help to fill in our sense of a character. Students should be encouraged to predict, to make sensible guesses. As students work on predictions, these discussion questions can be used to guide them: What are some of the ways to predict? What is the process of a sophisticated reader's thinking and predicting? What clues does an author give us to help us in making our predictions? Why are some predictions more likely than others?

A predicting chart is for students to record their predictions. As each subsequent chapter is discussed, you can review and correct previous predictions. This procedure serves to focus on predictions and to review the stories.

Use the facts and ideas the author gives.

Use your own knowledge.

Use new information that may cause you to change your mind.

Predictions:

_____

_____

_____

_____

Prediction Chart

What characters have we met so far?	What is the conflict in the story?	What are your predictions?	Why did you make those predictions?

Story Map

Characters _____

_____

_____

_____

Setting

Problem

Time and Place _____

_____

_____

Goal

_____

_____

Beginning ———▶ Development ———▶ Outcome

Episodes

_____

_____

_____

_____

Resolution

_____

_____

_____

_____

Using Character Webs—In the Novel Unit Approach

Attribute Webs are simply a visual representation of a character from the novel. They provide a systematic way for the students to organize and recap the information they have about a particular character. Attribute webs may be used after reading the novel to recapitulate information about a particular character or completed gradually as information unfolds, done individually, or finished as a group project.

One type of character attribute web uses these divisions:

- How a character acts and feels.
  (How does the character feel in this picture? How would you feel if this happened to you? How do you think the character feels?)

- How a character looks.
  (Close your eyes and picture the character. Describe him to me.)

- Where a character lives.
  (Where and when does the character live?)

- How others feel about the character.
  (How does another specific character feel about our character?)

In group discussion about the student attribute webs and specific characters, the teacher can ask for backup proof from the novel. You can also include inferential thinking.
Attribute webs need not be confined to characters. They may also be used to organize information about a concept, object or place.

Attribute Web

The attribute web below is designed to help you gather clues the author provides about what a character is like. Fill in the blanks with words and phrases which tell how the character acts and looks, as well as what the character says and what others say about him or her.

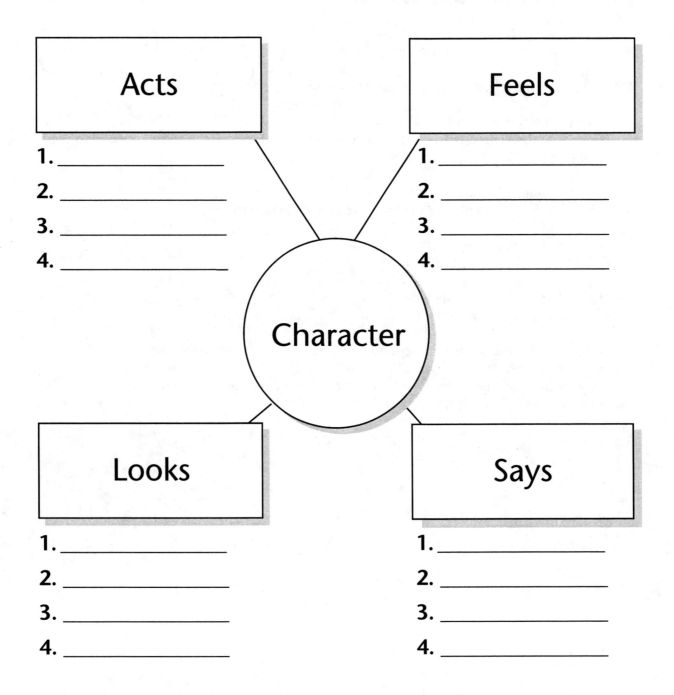

Attribute Web

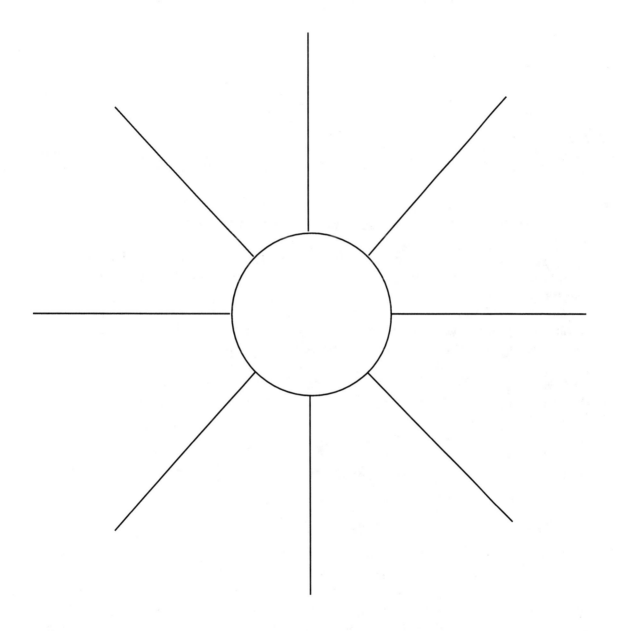

Chapter-by-Chapter
Vocabulary, Discussion Questions, and Activities

Chapter I   **"Stillwater"—Pages 3-8**

Chapter Summary
Mr. Popper returns home from a day's job of painting. Mrs. Popper is worrying about not having enough money for the winter when there is not much work for Mr. Popper.

Vocabulary
calcimine 3	untidy 3	absent-minded 5	expeditions 6
authority on the subject 6		bungalow 7	litter 8

Discussion Questions and Activities
1. Why is the chapter titled "Stillwater"? *(page 3, location of the story)*

2. Why do you think Mr. Popper is an unusual character? How does he differ from your father? What does your father do in his spare time? Why do you think Mr. Popper didn't get a winter time job? *(Answers will vary.)*

3. What examples can you find to prove Mr. Popper was absent-minded? *(Page 5, He painted three sides of a kitchen green and the other side yellow. He dreamed about far-away countries.)*

4. Locate some of the countries and places Mr. Popper dreamed about: a) India; b) the Himalayas; c) the South Seas; and d) the North and South Poles. Mark these on your world map.

5. What strange places and adventures do you dream about? What are the chances that you will ever go to these countries or have such an adventure? In pairs during class, share your answers.

6. How does one become "an authority on the subject"? *(page 6)*

7. Why didn't Mr. Popper work all year? *(Page 7, Most house painting and decorating in the colder parts of the United States is done in the spring and summer.)*

8. Why didn't Mrs. Popper like Mr. Popper's work? *(Page 8, It was "hard to sweep with a man sitting around reading all day," and she worried about not having enough money for food.)* What solutions would you find for Mrs. Popper's money problem? *(examples: second job for Mr. Popper or Mrs. Popper could work)*

Prediction
How do you think the Poppers will handle the money problem?

Literary Analysis: Characterization

Explain that characterization is the way an author informs readers about what characters are like. Direct characterization is when the author describes the character. Indirect characterization is when the reader figures out what the character is like based on what the character thinks, says, or does—or what other characters say about him or her.

Ask: "What are your impressions of Mr. Popper so far?" Ask students to support any words or phrases they use to describe him with evidence from the story. Have them jot down the evidence on a web like this one. For each of the major characters in this novel, make a character web.

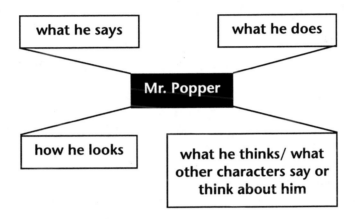

Literary Analysis: Humor

1. Can you list five things that kids think are funny but adults do not?

2. What are all the ways adults are funnier than kids?

3. Would you rather see something funny or hear something funny? Why?

4. Write your definition of humor.

Supplementary Activities

1. Story Map

Many stories have the same parts—a setting, a problem, a goal, and a series of events that lead to an ending or conclusion. These story elements can be placed on a story map. Just as a road map helps a driver get from one place to another, so, too, a story map leads a reader from one point to another. After reading the first chapter, what information do you have?

• What is the setting?
• Who is the main character?
• What is the problem? (This may change as the story progresses, so additional problems may be added.)

Begin the story map on page 12 of this guide.

2. Begin the research project on Antarctica on page 19 of this guide. Use books on the library table and the Internet.
Answers for the research project: 1. ice 2. 5,400,000 square miles 3. South Atlantic Ocean, Indian Ocean, Widely Sea, Ross Sea, South Pacific Ocean 4. South America 5. Mt. Erebus 6. Roald Amundsen and Robert F. Scott and their crews 7. seals, whales, birds, krill and fish 8. thick layer of ice and snow

Chapter II   "The Voice in the Air"—Pages 9-14

Chapter Summary
Mr. and Mrs. Popper discuss Antarctica. Mrs. Popper does not think she would like it at all, but Mr. Popper has written to the leader of an expedition to tell him how much he enjoyed the information about an earlier trip. Mr. Popper listens to a special broadcast from Antarctica, where Captain Drake says "Hello" to him and promises him a surprise.

Vocabulary
spectacles 10	prospect 10	erect 11	tidy 12
heathen 12	impressed 14		

Discussion Questions and Activities
1. Before reading the chapter: Titles of books and chapters are very important. What do you think this chapter title means? (Predictions—List on the board before the chapter is read. Compare after reading.)

2. How did Mr. and Mrs. Popper's views about the South Pole differ? *(Page 10, Mr. Popper never got tired of reading about the South Pole, but he thought that going there would be even better than just reading about it. Mrs. Popper thought that the South Pole sounded "very dull and cold, with all that ice and snow.")* Do you think you would like to visit the South Pole? Would you think visiting the Moon or Mars would be more interesting?

3. How did Mr. and Mrs. Popper's views about pets differ? *(Pages 11-12, Mr. Popper thought it would be fun to have a penguin for a pet. Mrs. Popper did not want any pets because pets make too much of a mess in the house and it costs money to feed a pet.)* How do your parents feel about pets?

4. What facts about penguins did Mr. Popper list? Are these facts true? *(Pages 11-12, Penguins do not fly like other birds. Penguins walk erect like men. They slide on their stomachs. They are very intelligent. Sea leopards eat penguins. All penguins live at the South Pole—not true.)*

Research Project

Antarctica

1. What covers almost all of this island?

2. What is the area of this continent?

3. Label the bodies of water surrounding Antarctica on the map.

4. What is the continent closest to Antarctica?

5. What is the name of Antarctica's most active volcano?

6. Two explorers claim to be the first to see Antarctica. Who are they?

7. What living creatures beside penguins are found in Antarctica?

8. What is an ice cap?

5. Why was the chapter titled "The Voice in the Air"? Can you think of another title for this chapter?

6. Why was Mr. Popper excited about the radio program from the South Pole? *(Page 14, He had written to Admiral Drake, and the explorer mentioned Mr. Popper's name on the radio and promised him a surprise.)*

Prediction
What will the surprise be?

Supplementary Activities
1. Complete the dialogue page on page 21 of this guide.

2. Role play Mr. and Mrs. Popper's discussion about Antarctica.

Chapter III   "Out of the Antarctic"—Pages 15-21

Chapter Summary
Mr. Popper receives a present—a penguin—from Admiral Drake.

Vocabulary

meekly 16	peace of mind 16	receipt 17	examined 17
dry ice 17	debris 18	extremely 18	

Discussion Questions and Activities
1. Why was Mr. Popper restless after the radio program? *(Page 15, The excitement of having Admiral Drake speak to him over the radio and his curiosity of Admiral Drake's message to him made Mr. Popper restless.)* What kind of surprises do you think that Admiral Drake might send?

2. What kind of package did Mr. Popper receive? Just from the outside of the box what might Mr. Popper have surmised about the contents? *(Page 17, It was covered with markings such as "UNPACK AT ONCE" and "KEEP COOL." There were air holes, so whatever was inside the box might be alive. There was a layer of dry ice, and there were noises coming from the box.)*

3. What is another way to say, "Mr. Popper was speechless with delight"? *(page 18)*

4. How did the penguin react to Mr. Popper's house? *(Page 18, The penguin made "Ork" noises and jumped over the packing debris. He was a curious visitor.)* Where did this penguin come from? Had it been living in captivity, or did Admiral Drake capture it and immediately send it to Mr. Popper? Would that make any difference?

5. Make a list of words to describe the penguin. *(page 18)*

Using Dialogue

Directions

Choose a bit of dialogue from the book to investigate. Fill in the chart to describe this way of writing and telling a story.

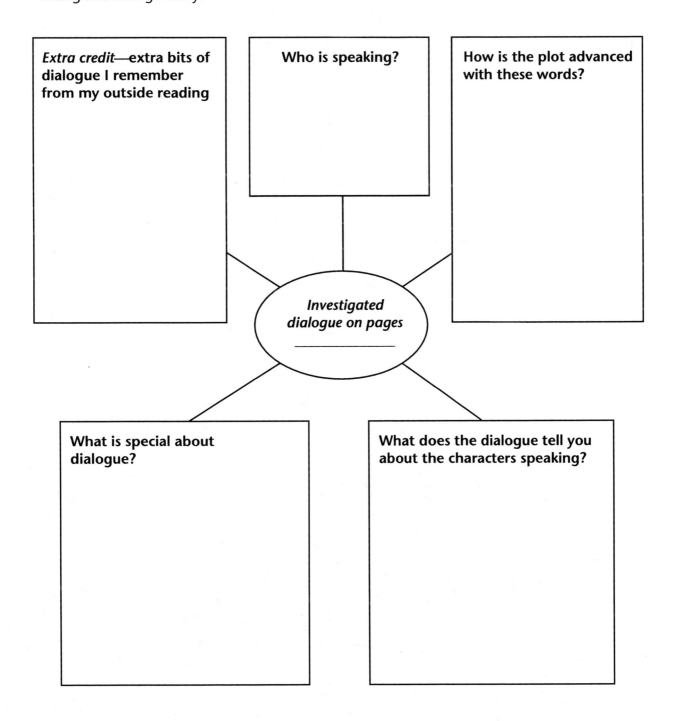

| *Extra credit*—extra bits of dialogue I remember from my outside reading | Who is speaking? | How is the plot advanced with these words? |

Investigated dialogue on pages _____

| What is special about dialogue? | What does the dialogue tell you about the characters speaking? |

6. Why did Mr. Popper call the penguin Captain Cook? *(Page 21, The penguin made the sound, "Gook.")*

7. How will Captain Cook's survival with the Poppers be different than its struggle to survive in Antarctica?

Prediction
How will the Popper family manage Captain Cook? What do you think will be necessary for Captain Cook to survive in Stillwater?

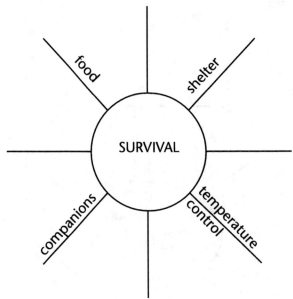

Supplementary Activities
  1. Research
   Research penguins. Complete the chart on the next page of this guide.

  2. Venn Diagram
   Using a Venn diagram, compare Captain Cook's survival in the wild and survival with the Popper family.

Penguins

Type	Height	Weight	Where it Lives	Special Characteristics	Unusual Facts
King Penguin					
Adelie Penguin					
African Penguin					
Chinstrap Penguin					
Emperor Penguin					
Galapagos Penguin					
Gentoo Penguin					
Little Blue Penguin					
Magellanic Penguin					
Rockhopper Penguin					
Royal Penguin					
Yellow-Eyed Penguin					

3. Writing:
- Write Mr. Popper's thank you letter to Admiral Drake.

- Pretend you are Captain Cook. You have just gotten out of the shipping crate and are looking around in Mr. Popper's house. What do you notice? How do you feel about this new habitat? Are you disturbed by anything? How do you feel about living with humans? What do you fear?

Chapter IV  "Captain Cook"—Pages 22-30

Chapter Summary

Captain Cook begins to make himself at home in the Poppers' house. To find out what Captain Cook would eat, the Poppers took out all the food in their icebox; however, the only food he was interested in was the goldfish in their bowl. Captain Cook moved into the empty icebox and the Poppers had to find another place for their food.

Vocabulary

suitable 23	surveying 23	retreating 23	curiosity 23
circular 23	pompously 23	solemnly 26	trilled 26
waddled 28			

Discussion Questions and Activities

1. Who was the original Captain Cook for whom the penguin was named? *(Page 22, Captain James Cook was an English seafarer, 1728-1779.)*

2. How did the Poppers try to find out what Captain cook would eat? *(Pages 25-28, They put the food from the icebox on the table. He looked all of it over and went into the other room and ate all the goldfish.)*

3. The Poppers had an icebox. How does an icebox differ from a refrigerator? Do we have iceboxes today? When was this book published? When did refrigerators become common in the United States?

4. How many of these statements about Mr. Popper's penguin could be based on truth about penguins? Research:
   a) Page 26, "...penguins can go for a month without food."
   b) Page 28, Captain Cook swallowed the last goldfish.
   c) Page 29, Captain Cook was going to sleep in the refrigerator.
   d) Page 30, "Penguins make their nests of pebbles and stones."

Prediction
What do you think the troubles in Chapter V will be?

Supplementary Activities
1. Design a cool house for Captain Cook. Make a drawing and explain how you will lower the temperature. At what temperature do zoos keep the penguins' habitat?

2. Research penguins in zoos. If possible, visit a zoo and learn about penguins. Prepare a list of questions about penguins that you would like the zoo keepers to answer.

Chapter V   "Troubles with a Penguin"—Pages 31-37

Chapter Summary
Mr. Popper has problems getting the service man to fix the icebox for Captain Cook.

Vocabulary

eventful 31	license 31	ventilating 32	bored 32
unsympathetic 32	indignantly 33	remodeled 36	promptly 36

Discussion Questions and Activities
1. Why did Mr. Popper feel sad about paying the service man for holes drilled in the icebox? *(Page 33, He did not even have much money to buy beans and food for his family, much less holes in the ice box.)*

2. Why do you think the service man was so unsympathetic? *(Answers will vary.)*

3. Research: Can penguins be trained like Captain Cook to use a refrigerator?

Prediction
Why would a policeman come to the Poppers' house?

Supplementary Activity
Role play Mr. Popper and the service man.

Chapter VI   "More Troubles"—Pages 38-43

Chapter Summary
A policeman comes to the Poppers' house to inquire about the animal that frightened the service man. He tells Mr. Popper to inquire at the city offices about a pet license for a penguin.

Vocabulary

dignity 38	municipal ordinance 40	distinctly 42	outraged 42

Discussion Questions and Activities

1. Who complained to the police about Captain Cook? *(page 39, the service man)*

2. What troubles did Mr. Popper have getting a license for Captain Cook. List in sequence.

   Page 40—The policeman did not know about the municipal ordinance about penguins.

   Page 41—Mr. Popper called City Hall.

   Page 41—No one seemed to understand that Captain Cook was a penguin.

   Page 42—They thought Captain Cook wanted a license to shoot birds, and it was the wrong season.

   Page 43—The Automobile License Bureau thought Mr. Popper wanted a car license.

3. Was this chapter funny or not? Why? An author uses certain elements to create humor or to make us laugh. These elements are:

   —word play and nonsense-coined words, absurd names, puns
   —surprise and the unexpected
   —exaggeration
   —ridicule
   —unusual comparisons

   Students may compare what they think is funny in this book. They will not all agree on what is funny. The teacher begins a list of "funnies" and adds to this list after each chapter.

Supplementary Activity
With a partner, write and record a song that gives the feeling of the novel.

Chapter VII   "Captain Cook Builds A Nest"—Pages 44-49

Chapter Summary
Captain Cook helps Mrs. Popper pick up the house by taking scattered things to the icebox. Mr. Popper dresses up to take Captain Cook out for a walk.

Vocabulary

reluctantly 44	belatedly 44	prowled 45	thoroughness 45
subdued 45	astonishment 46	harmonica 48	consumed 48
rookery 48	heathen 49		

Discussion Questions and Activities

1. What did Captain Cook collect and why did he do this? *(Pages 47-48, He collected thread, a white chess bishop, six parts of a jig saw puzzle, a teaspoon, matches, a radish, two pennies, a nickel, and many other small objects.)*

2. Why did Mrs. Popper think the penguin could be good to have around? *(page 49, for keeping the house picked up)*

3. Why do you think Mr. Popper dressed up to exercise Captain Cook? *(Answers will vary.)*

Chapter VIII   "Penguin's Promenade"—Pages 50-56

Chapter Summary
Mr. Popper and Captain Cook meet a neighbor carrying her groceries, a newspaper reporter, and a photographer on their walk around town.

Vocabulary

strutted 51	investigate 52	anteater 52	boric 53
mistook 53	vigorously 53	tripod 54	

Discussion Questions and Activities

1. In this chapter, find all the words that mean "walk." The class makes a list and then draws words and pantomimes.

2. "Is it [the penguin] a he or a she? The public will want to know." (page 54) Mr. Popper said the bird's name was Captain Cook. " 'That makes it a he,' said the reporter..." (page 55) Would this necessarily be true? Why or why not? Remember this story was written in 1938. How have things changed since 1938? What kind of female captains are there now? *(Answers will vary.)*

3. Do you think the reporters believed Mr. Popper's story about where he got the penguin? Why or why not? How could Mr. Popper have used the reporters to his advantage? *(Answers will vary.)*

Prediction
What problems will Mr. Popper have with Captain Cook? What possible problem is suggested at the end of this chapter? *(Page 56, "The man who kept the barbershop had, up to this time, been a very good friend of Mr. Popper's.")* What are the key words?

Supplementary Activities

1. Research pelicans. How are they like penguins? How are they different from penguins? Where do they live? What do they eat? How do they care for their young? Complete a Venn diagram of penguins and pelicans.

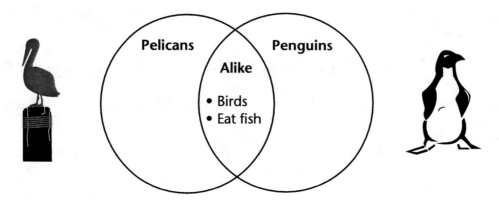

2. Write the story the reporter might write about Mr. Popper and Captain Cook. Make sure there is a headline. The story may be illustrated.

Chapter IX   "In the Barber Shop"—Pages 57-61

Chapter Summary
Captain Cook disrupts activity in the barber shop and is asked to leave by the barber. Mr. Popper and Captain Cook exit through the back door.

Vocabulary

spectacle 57	amid 59	absolutely 59	unwearyingly 60
exhausted 61			

Discussion Questions and Activities

1. How did Mr. Popper explain penguins' reasons for climbing? *(Page 60, They can't fly but they have to go up in the air somehow.)*

2. How do penguins go downstairs? *(Page 60, They toboggan whenever they get a chance.)* How did that affect Mr. Popper? *(Page 61, He slid down three flights of stairs with Captain Cook.)* How could Mr. Popper have avoided sliding down the stairs? *(Answers will vary.)*

3. How did Captain Cook and Mr. Popper relax after their exercise? *(Page 61, Mr. Popper went to lie down and Captain Cook had a shower and took a nap in the icebox.)* How do you suppose Captain Cook changed Mrs. Popper's routine in the kitchen? Where did she put the food she used to keep in the icebox? Did Mr. Popper make a mess when he took a shower? Did he leave a water trail from the tub to the icebox? *(Answers will vary.)*

Prediction
Look at the cover of the book again. What do you think is going to happen in this book?

Supplementary Activities
1. Draw a four part sequence of the actions of this chapter.

2. Retell the actions of this chapter from Mrs. Popper's viewpoint.

Chapter X  "Shadows"—Pages 62-67

Chapter Summary
Captain Cook becomes ill and is no longer friendly. Mr. Popper has a veterinary doctor examine Captain Cook, but with no success. Next, Mr. Popper writes to an aquarium about Captain Cook. The curator also has a sick penguin who may be suffering from loneliness. He sends Mr. Popper another penguin.

Vocabulary

rotogravure 62	sulking 63	mopey 63	stupor 66
solemn 66	despair 66		

Discussion Questions and Activities
1. How did Captain Cook show he was very ill? *(Pages 62-63, He didn't act happy, wouldn't play, his coat lost its gloss, and he had a high temperature.)*

2. Why did the veterinary doctor think this was a hopeless case? *(Page 64, Stillwater didn't have the right climate for a penguin to thrive.)*

3. What did the veterinary prescribe? *(page 64, sherbet and ice packs)* What would you prescribe? What does your mother give you if you have a temperature?

4. How did the Poppers get the second sick penguin? *(Pages 66-67, Mr. Popper wrote to the head of an aquarium, who also had a sick but possibly lonely penguin. He sent his penguin, Greta, to live with Captain Cook.)*

Prediction
What do you think will happen when Greta makes her home with the Poppers?

Supplementary Activities
1. Write a poem about sick Captain Cook.

2. Draw a before and after portrait of the sick Captain Cook.

Chapter XI   "Greta"—Pages 68-73

Chapter Summary
Mrs. Popper complains about not having an icebox for food. The weather is getting much colder because it is winter. Mr. Popper decides to turn off the heat in the house and opens the windows for the penguins. Next he runs water on the house floor and it freezes. Then snow comes in the windows. The penguins thrive, but Mrs. Popper is not pleased.

Vocabulary
squirming 69   tremendously 72

Discussion Questions and Activities
1. What unusual decisions did Mr. Popper make in this chapter? *(pages 69-72, marking the penguins' names with white paint, making the penguins comfortable in the house, making an indoor ice rink)* What decisions would you have made? Your decisions may be real-life type decisions or closer to the fantastic ones Mr. Popper made. Be ready to share your decisions and justify them.

2. Do you think the Poppers' neighbors knew what was happening in the neighborhood? *(Answers will vary.)*

3. Why did the Popper children and Mrs. Popper put up with such wild actions? Would your mother? Why or why not? *(Answers will vary.)*

Prediction
How will Mr. Popper solve his problem of the melting ice rink and keep the penguins happy and healthy?

Supplementary Activity
In Chapter XI the penguins have a skating rink in the Poppers' living room. Mr. Popper opens the windows and snowdrifts are in the living room. Have students reread the descriptions. Draw the indoor winter scene on art paper and color thoroughly with crayon. Using large paint brushes and diluted white tempera paint, have students whitewash their papers to lend a snowy effect to the art work.

Chapter XII   "More Mouths to Feed"—Pages 74-80

Chapter Summary
Mr. Popper moves the penguins to the basement and has a freezing plant installed. Instead of sitting in the living room, Mr. Popper would read in the basement, while wearing his winter coat and mittens. The penguins have changed the Poppers' lives.

Vocabulary
refrigerating 75   credit 75   droll 76   tremendous 77
unfortunately 78   spar 78

Discussion Questions and Activities
1. How did Greta and Captain Cook change the living arrangements at the Poppers'? *(Page 74, The furnace was moved to the living room. A freezing plant was placed in the cellar.)*

2. Research: What is the normal penguin body temperature? Why did Mr. Popper need to know this? *(page 75, so he could keep the penguin eggs at the right temperature for hatching)*

3. What makes this definitely not a realistic story? *(Answers will vary.)* Look at your realistic and fantasy story chart. Where do the actions in this chapter fit? Be ready to support your point of view.

4. Mr. Popper made some changes in this basement. What were they? *(Pages 78-79, He dug a large hole in the cellar floor for swimming and diving and flooded a section of the cellar for an ice rink.)*

5. How had Mr. Popper's life changed? Do you think it had improved? Why or why not?

Predictions
What serious problems will Mr. Popper have now? Look at the next chapter title, "Money Worries." What has caused this problem? How do you think Mr. Popper will find the money for supporting his big family?

Supplementary Activity
Research: What is the normal penguin body temperature? How many eggs do the various kinds of penguins lay? Who takes care of the eggs? How do zoos handle penguin eggs? What do penguins weigh at birth? How long does it take for a penguin to mature? Can you figure out what species these penguins might be? Use the process of elimination. Resource: encyclopedias and books on a library table.

Chapter XIII   "Money Worries"—Pages 81-84

Chapter Summary
Mr. Popper has an idea to solve the money problem—the penguins will put on their acts in theaters.

Vocabulary
practically 82   droll 84   portable 84

Discussion Questions and Activities
1. Problems change in many stories, but what was the one problem that seemed to stay with the Poppers? *(page 81, lack of money)*

2. What were the solutions that the Poppers suggested? *(pages 82-83, eat the penguins, sell the penguins, train the penguins to act in theaters)*

3. Why did Mrs. Popper play the piano with her gloves on? *(Page 84, It was cold in the cellar.)* Can a person really play the piano while wearing gloves?

4. How had the penguins changed the Poppers' lives? Was the change for the better or worse? Support your opinion. *(Answers will vary.)*

Prediction
How will the Poppers get the penguins on stage?

Supplementary Activities
1. Research: How many pounds of fish do grown penguins eat each day? Look in your newspaper or grocery store for the price of fresh fish per pound. How much would it cost to feed one penguin for one day? for a week? How much might it cost to feed the penguin family? Would it be cheaper to feed the penguins canned shrimp and other canned fish? Price canned shrimp and other canned fish at the store. Notice the weight of each can. How many cans would an adult penguin eat? Make a chart of your findings.

2. Research: How are seals trained? Can penguins really be trained?

3. Music Activity: Play the three songs Mrs. Popper played for training the penguins.

Chapter XIV   "Mr. Greenbaum"—Pages 85-91

Chapter Summary
The Popper family and the penguins get on a bus to go for an interview at a theater.

Vocabulary
astonished 88	protest 88	complaints 89	succeeded 89
solemn 90			

Discussion Questions and Activities
1. What were the obstacles Mr. Popper faced getting the penguins on stage? *(Pages 88-89, They had to get to the theater, bus fare had to be figured for the birds, the penguins had to have cold air on the bus, and the passengers complained about the birds.)*

2. Mr. Greenbaum had a suggestion for the name of the act. What would you call it? What would you write on the theater marquee or program? What ad would you run in the paper?

Supplementary Activity
Role play what the passengers on the bus said about the penguins.

Chapter XV   "Popper's Performing Penguins"—Pages 92-100

Chapter Summary
Popper's Performing Penguins are called on to substitute for an act that did not arrive on time for a performance. They do an outstanding job and are offered a contract.

Vocabulary

rehearse 93	indulgence 93	novelty 93	unforeseen
circumstances 93	dignified 93	formations 94	precision 94
prostrate 97	confusion 98	absolutely unique 99	sensation 99
troupers 99			

Discussion Questions and Activities
1. Why were the Popper Penguins given a chance to perform? *(Page 92, The Marvelous Marcos had not appeared.)*

2. How would you say: "Ladies and gentlemen, with your kind indulgence…Owing to unforeseen circumstances…"? *(page 93)*

3. How were the penguins like real actors? *(Pages 94-98, They drilled with precision, had a sparring contest, pretended to fight and knock down, and could adapt to the circumstances.)*

Supplementary Activities
1. Math: How much money had you figured it would take to feed the penguins? What other expenses do you think have to be planned for? Will the penguins stay in hotels? What problems will that cause?

2. Drama: Pantomime the act of Mr. and Mrs. Popper and the penguins.

Chapter XVI   "On The Road"—Pages 101-107

Chapter Summary
The Penguins are an outstanding hit in the theater.

Vocabulary

observation platform 103	gasping 103	Pullmans 103	berths 103
ecstatic 103	broadening 104	riotous 106	interfered 107

Discussion Questions and Activities

1. What do you think the Poppers had to do to prepare for the tour with the penguins? *(pages 101-102)*

2. If you were Mr. Popper, how would you have taken the birds through the whole length of the train? *(page 103)*

3. The penguins interfered with other acts on the stage. How could Mr. Popper have prevented this? What do you think the owners or the performers in the other acts said to Mr. Popper after the show? *(pages 106-107)*

Prediction

Do you think the penguins are going to continue to perform for the rest of their lives? What kind of ending would you write for this story?

Supplementary Activities

1. There are many terms about riding on the train in this chapter. Make a comparison chart of children in the class who have ridden on trains, planes and busses.

2. Research: There are three "train words" in the vocabulary. See how many other "train words" you know. Look in the train books on the library table.

3. Research: How do children in show business handle the problems of school and truant officers?

Chapter XVII   "Fame"—Pages 108-114

Chapter Summary

There were certain advantages given to the penguins because they were famous. The shrimp company gave them free shrimp. As the season moved along it became increasingly difficult to keep the penguins cool.

Vocabulary

celebrated 108	startled 111	nuisance 112	testimonial 112
irritable 114			

Discussion Questions and Activities

1. It was not easy to discipline the penguins. List all the embarrassing situations that they brought to Mr. Popper so far in the book. Could each of these situations have been prevented? How would you have tried to avoid these problems?

   page 52—On his walk, Captain Cook investigated the stockings under Mrs. Callahan's dress.

   page 59—poor behavior at the barbershop

page 89—riding the bus with the windows open
pages 102-103—the taxi drivers' accident
page 103—getting the penguins from one end of the train to the other
page 104—climbing ladders to the upper berths
page 107—disturbing the high wire act
page 108-110—annoying the opera singer
page 111—riding elevators too often
page 111—biting the brass buttons off a bell-boy's uniform
page 112—tying up traffic when they went for walks

Prediction
Will life for Mr. Popper and the penguins be better back in Stillwater?

Supplementary Activities
1. Research: When were escalators invented?

2. Writing: What would have happened if there had been escalators in the hotels where the penguins stayed? Write an extra chapter about the penguins tobogganing down escalators.

Chapter XVIII

"April Winds"—Pages 115-122

Chapter Summary
Mr. Popper and the penguins are getting worn out, and it is getting very warm for them. Mr. Popper takes the penguins to the wrong theater because he did not sleep much the night before. The penguins are on the same stage as the seals who like to eat penguins. The fire and the police departments come to the rescue and none of the penguins are injured. The theater manager is very angry and he gets a warrant for Mr. Popper's arrest.

Vocabulary
burly 117	shudder 118	vexed 119	warrant 121
daze 121			

Discussion Questions and Activities
1. Why do you think Mr. Popper had all these troubles in this chapter? *(Pages 116-122, He was nervous and stayed up most of the night giving the penguins showers. He needed his sleep. He gave the name of the wrong theater to the taxi driver.)*

2. How did the police and firemen solve the problems between the seals and penguins? *(Page 119, They gave their helmets and caps to them and the animals were distracted.)*

3. Why were the penguins taken to the police station? *(Pages 121-122, They went to the wrong theater and disturbed the acts that were scheduled and the audience.)*

Prediction
Who will rescue Mr. Popper and his penguins?

Supplementary Activities
1. **Research**
    Do seals eat penguins?

2. **Research**
    When was air conditioning invented? When did it become common in hotels and theaters? How would air conditioning have helped Mr. Popper and his penguins?

Chapter XIX   "Admiral Drake"—Pages 123-131

Chapter Summary
Admiral Drake returns from his expedition and bails Mr. Popper and the penguins out of jail. Mr. Klein from a film company makes an offer to make movies of the Poppers' penguins, and Admiral Drake also makes an offer.

Vocabulary

presentable 126	accustomed 126	Easy Street 130	outwit 131

Discussion Questions and Activities
1. What is bail? *(the security or guaranty given or agreed upon to release or obtain the release of a person under arrest)*

2. How much bail money were the police demanding? *(page 123, $500—Mr. Popper; $1200—twelve birds; total $1700)* Who posted bail for Mr. Popper and the penguins? *(pages 126-127, Admiral Drake)*

3. Why did Admiral Drake think explorers preferred the South Pole to the North Pole? *(Page 129, They liked the company of penguins at the South Pole.)* Why do you think Admiral Drake proposed taking the penguins to the North Pole?

4. Mr. Popper had two business propositions to consider. As a class, vote and give Mr. Popper a consensus of your opinions.

    —put the penguins in the movies
    —take the penguins to the North Pole

Prediction
What could happen to the penguins if they become movie stars? Or what could happen to them if they move to the North Pole?

Literary Analysis: Conflict

Conflict is structure that drives the plot. There are three main types: Person vs. Person, Person vs. Nature or Society, and Person vs. Himself or Herself (inner conflict). Analyze the main conflicts in *Mr. Popper's Penguins*. Where do you find inner conflict? Can you find examples of each of the three types of conflict?

Supplementary Activities

1. Research
Have any penguins been moved to the North Pole?

2. Nature of Conflict
Complete the Nature of Conflict chart on the next page of this guide.

Chapter XX   "Farewell, Mr. Popper"—Pages 132-139

Chapter Summary
Mr. Popper makes the decision that the penguins should go to the North Pole. After Mr. Popper has said his sad goodbyes to the penguins, Admiral Drake insists that Mr. Popper come with him on his expedition to the North Pole. Mrs. Popper and the children agree that this is a good thing and they will miss him, but that they can manage.

Vocabulary
haggard 132   reputation 136   contribution to science 136

Discussion Questions and Activities

1. How did Mr. Popper satisfy both Mr. Klein and Admiral Drake? *(Pages 133-134, He agreed to the making a short movie and to sending the birds with Admiral Drake.)*

2. How much would the $25,000 of 1938 be worth today? What are the various ways you could find this information? *(bank, library, estimation)*

	1938	1997
**ice cream cone	$ .05	$ 1.50
**house	$5,000	$150,000
**small Ford car	$ 750	$ 15,000

3. Why do you think a trip to the North Pole was a surprise to Mr. Popper? *(Answers will vary.)*

4. Do you think most wives would accept this trip like Mrs. Popper did? Why or why not? *(Answers will vary.)*

The Nature of Conflict

As is true in real life, the characters in novels face many conflicts. When two people or forces struggle over the same thing, conflict occurs. The excitement in novels develops from the use of the three main types of conflict: (1) person against person; (2) person against nature or society; and (3) person against himself or herself.

Below list some of the conflicts from the novel. In the space provided, briefly describe the conflict and indicate which type of conflict is involved, writing "PP" for person vs. person, "PN" for person vs. nature or society, and "PS" for person vs. self. Then choose three of the conflicts and describe how each was resolved.

Conflict	Description	Type

Conflict #1 resolution: _____

Conflict #2 resolution: _____

Conflict #3 resolution: _____

Literary Analysis: Theme

Theme is an important idea that emerges from a story. The authors usually don't state the theme of a work outright, but let their readers decide for themselves what ideas in the story are the most important. For clues to them, readers can look at the characters, the main events, and the conflicts in a story. You should also take a close look at what the main characters learn and how they change from the beginning of the story to the end. Most stories have several themes. With a small group, brainstorm some possible themes of *Mr. Popper's Penguins*. The diagram below should help you get started.

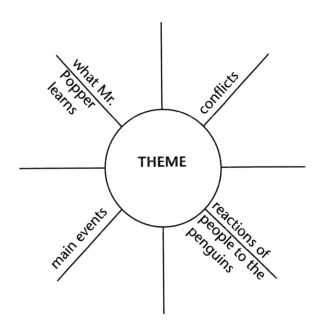

What do you think is the most important thing to remember about this story?

Some Universal Themes in Literature:
• family relationships
• search for dreams
• courage
• man's relationship with nature

Support your ideas for the theme or themes with examples from the novel.

© Novel Units, Inc.

39

Postreading Questions

1. Summarize the story using the story diagram below. What purpose is there in a story diagram? How would using a story diagram help an author?

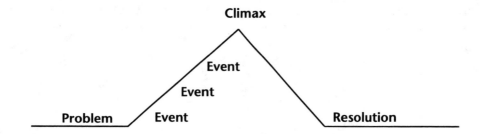

2. Plot: In literature the plot often is carried along by causes and effects of decisions made by the main characters. Had a character made an alternate decision, the plot would have turned in a different direction. What were the important decisions or turning points in this story? What if Mr. Popper had not written the letter about the sick penguin and Greta had not come? What if Mr. Popper did not make the basement into a winter spot for the penguins? What if the penguins had not gotten into the theater business?

3. Setting: How important is the setting to the story? (In what time and place is the story set?) How do the various settings contribute to the mood and move the plot along? Describe the settings in *Mr. Popper's Penguins* and how they are connected with the major ideas of the novel.

4. Does the plot seem unrealistic? Were any events out of place or contrived? Did you find that any parts lost your attention? Would you change anything about this story? What would you say to the authors about this book, if you met them signing books in a bookstore?

5. If you were to place yourself in the book, who would you be and where would you come in?

6. If you were making a one-hour video based on the story, which episodes would you include—and which would you leave out? Why?

7. What other titles could you think of for this novel?

8. Which chapter is your favorite?

9. Was there any part of this story that you especially liked or disliked?

Postreading Extension Activities

Writing

1. Write a character sketch in which you describe Mr. Popper.

   a) Prewriting: Jot down ideas for your sketch on an attribute web.
   b) Writing: Begin by describing your impressions of Mr. Popper in detail. Illustrate your description by referring to what he says and does. You might want to choose the episode in the story that shows you the most about him. Make sure you "show" your readers what Mr. Popper is like—don't just "tell" them.

2. Write three journal entries Mr. Popper might have made at different points in the novel.

3. Respond to this story by writing a cinquain that describes Mr. Popper.

> Mr. Popper
> Adjective, adjective
> Verb-ing, verb-ing, verb-ing
> Four words (your choice)
> Noun that describes what or who Mr. Popper is

4. Have the students rewrite a chapter for Reader's Theater. (The narrative is changed into dialogue, with short pieces of narration when necessary.) Students sit in a circle with name tags or simple costumes/props. Chapters XI and XIII are two particularly suitable chapters.

5. Write a letter from Mr. Popper to his family from the North Pole. How are the penguins adapting to their new life? What has Mr. Popper learned that he never found in books?

Listening and Speaking Activities

1. Stage a TV interview with some of the central characters in the story. For homework, students playing each role gather impressions about what their character is like. Other students make lists of interview questions.

2. Retell an episode from your favorite chapter from the viewpoint of another character, e.g. the barber, Mrs. Popper.

3. Work with a partner to write an imaginary dialogue between yourself and one of the characters in the novel. The character you choose should act and respond in the same manner as he or she does in the novel. With your partner present your dialogue for the class.

Art

1. Read several of the descriptive selections on the following pages from the book: Pages 18, 20-21, 23-24, 45, 63, 76-77, 106-107 and 119-121. Have the class listen carefully for descriptive details, such as size, color, texture and number. Illustrate the descriptive selections.

2. Divide a sheet of drawing paper in four sections. What are the main parts of the story? Class members may disagree. Illustrate. Another version of this activity is a class mural of the novel. It is a great way to summarize the novel or be used as a culminating activity.

3. Choose part of the story which is not illustrated, but which you feel should be. Illustrate it.

4. Robert Lawson is the illustrator. He has worked on many books. Can you find the titles? Does he use the same style or techniques in his other books?

5. Create a shoe box diorama to illustrate a scene from the book. (Materials might include: plastic figures, wrapping paper scraps, styrofoam, popsicle sticks, etc.) Write a three or four sentence summary of what is shown.

6. Design a poster encouraging people to visit Antarctica.

Bibliography of Penguin Books

Nonfiction

Arnold, Caroline. *Penguin*. New York: Morrow Junior Books, 1988.

Barkhausen, Annette. *Penguins*. Milwaukee: Gareth Stevens, 1994.

Barrett, Norman S. *Penguins*. New York: F. Watts, 1991.

Bernard. Robin. *Penguins: Theme Unit*. New York: Scholastic, 1994.

Davis, Lloyd Spence. *Penguin: A Season in the Life of the Adelie Penguin*. San Diego: Harcourt Brace, 1994.

Dewey, Jennifer. *Birds of Antarctic: The Adelie Penguin*. Boston: Little, Brown, 1989.

Fletcher, Neil. *Penguin*. Boston: Houghton Mifflin, 1993.

Fontanel, Beatrice. *The Penguin: A Funny Bird*. Watertown, MA: Charlesbridge Publishing, 1992.

Kalman, Bobbie. *Penguins*. New York: Crabtree, 1995.

McMillan, Bruce. *Penguins at Home: Gentoos of Antarctica*. Boston: Houghton Mifflin, 1993.

McMillan, Bruce. *Puffins Climb, Penguins Rhyme*. San Diego: Harcourt Brace, 1995.

Nagle, Robin. *Penguins*. New York: Gallery, 1990.

Ollason, Robert J. *Penguin Parade*. Minneapolis: Lerner Publications, 1995.

Paladino, Catherine. *Pomona: The Birth of a Penguin*. New York: F. Watts, 1991.

Patent, Dorothy Hinshaw. *Looking at Penguins*. New York: Holiday House, 1993.

Robinson, Claire. *Penguin*. Mahwah, N.J.: Troll Associates, 1994.

Stone, Lynn. *Penguins*. Vero Beach, FL: Rourke Enterprises, 1989.

Vernon, Adele. *The Hoiho, New Zealand's Yellow-eyed Penguin*. New York: Putnam, 1991.

Wexo, Jon Bonnett. *Penguins*. Mankato, MN; Creative Education, 1990.

Assessment for *Mr. Popper's Penguins*

Assessment is an on-going process, more than a quiz at the end of the book. Points may be added to show the level of achievement. When an item is completed, the teacher and the student check it.

Name _____   Date _____

Student   **Teacher**

_____   _____   1. Make an attribute web for Mr. Popper.

_____   _____   2. Give yourself one point for each vocabulary activity completed.

_____   _____   3. Make a list of the problems in the novel.

_____   _____   4. Choose one of the research projects. Prepare a presentation for the class using graphic organizers.

_____   _____   5. Change three things in this novel and explain how the changes would make a difference. Make a list of these changes and compare with a classmate's list. How would these changes affect the ending of the novel?

_____   _____   6. If you were an illustrator, what pictures would you add? Why? Use any type of media to make an illustration that you think would add to the novel. Write a paragraph explaining how this illustration would help the reader.

_____   _____   7. Complete the story map.

_____   _____   8. Complete the penguin chart.

_____   _____   9. Write three questions about the novel, and participate in a small group discussion of these and other student-generated questions.

_____   _____   10. Complete one of the suggested art projects.